Executive Producers: John Christianson and Ron Berry
Art Design: Gary Currant
Layout: Currant Design Group and Best Impression Graphics

HOW i FEEL

SCARED

by Marcia Leonard
illustrated by Bartholomew

This little girl doesn't like the dark.
She feels scared.

This little boy is scared, too.
There's a bug crawling on his arm.

These kids are afraid of the neighbor's dog.

Would he scare you, too?
Can you make a face that looks scared?

This little girl is scared of thunder,
but her big sister likes it.

Do loud noises frighten you?

This little boy climbed up high.
Now he's afraid to climb down.

Has that ever happened to you?
What would you do?

It's okay to be scared.
That scary feeling is your body's way
of telling you to be careful.

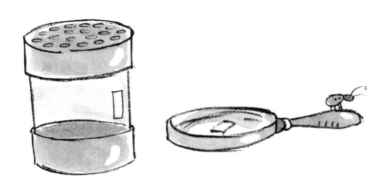

Sometimes it helps to learn about
what scares you.

Sometimes you can get used to it--
a little at a time.

And sometimes you can even
make friends with what scares you!

The most important thing
is to tell Mommy or Daddy
when you are scared,
because they can help you
make the scared feeling go away.

SIZING UP FEAR
Instructions

Use the Sizing-up-Fear activity found in the back of this book to help your child express the intensity of a particular fear. Remove the chart and reusable stickers from the pocket. Ask your child to choose any one of the fear stickers and place it in the white square on the chart. Then help your child use the other stickers to cover up the figure a little or a lot, depending on the size of his or her fear. For example, if bugs are only a little bit scary, cover just the figure's feet. If they're extremely scary, cover the whole body. Try this with other fear stickers. Talk about the size of different fears—and ways to make them smaller.